How To Write A White Paper In One Day

Everything you need to know to create your own powerful marketing tool.

by Brian Boys

- Learn the difference between white papers and other marketing tools
- Explore the benefits of writing your own
- Learn how to find published sources to bolster your argument
- Get step-by-step instructions for creating and polishing your document
- Includes the exclusive *White Paper In A Day Template*
- Find ideas for distributing your white paper once it's done

Table Of Contents

PART 1: Introduction To White Papers

Find out what makes white papers so powerful and why you might want to write your own.

You're Off To A Good Start Already

The fact that you're reading this introduction means you're interested in white papers. And you're at least willing to think about writing your own. That alone puts you ahead of about 95% of your colleagues.

You might have heard the stories about how a single white paper generated millions in sales for a software company. Or maybe you don't know much about them but are considering adding a white paper to your marketing mix. This brief book will give you a whirlwind introduction to the format and then a step-by-step method for writing your first white paper in a very short time.

What's So Special About White Papers?

First of all, there's nothing magic about a white paper. It's simply a report that's written to grab the reader's attention and gain their trust. (We'll look at a more formal definition when we get into where white papers came from.)

But what makes a white paper so *potentially* effective is that if you write it properly, it's more likely to be read by your prospects than a web page, brochure, or even a press release. More than any of those, a well-written white paper benefits the person reading it — regardless if they decide to do business with you.

If properly written, your white paper has a chance of accomplishing your dream scenario where your prospect takes it to a decision-making meeting and uses it as an argument in favor of choosing to do business with your company.

What's great about a white paper is that it promises the reader that he or she will learn something. In fact, in the method I'll take you through in this book, your title will address the solution to one of his or her biggest problems. It's information they will be seeking out. And they will come to you to find it.

Permission Marketing vs. Interruption Marketing

Interruption marketing is when you stop someone in the middle of something important to tell them about something they've expressed no interest in. Like interrupting someone while she's making dinner to talk about life insurance.

Permission marketing is when you provide information at your prospect's request. It's a dialogue rather than a one-sided conversation. You have to move at the prospect's pace, but you're much more likely to make the sale.

It's sort of like the Trojan war, where after ten years of unsuccessful assaults on the city, the Greeks gave the people of Troy exactly what they wanted—a giant horse. It was the Trojans who broke down their own walls and did all the work of dragging the horse into their city. Of course, you're not out to ravage your clients. But it shows how permission beats brute force any day.

"OK," you say, "I think my business could really use a white paper. I'll just hire somebody to write one for me."

How Much Would It Cost To Have Someone Write One For You?

If you were to hire professionals to write and design an eight page white paper, you could expect to pay anywhere from $3000 on up. Large organizations, which use their white papers to publish the results of original research, will spend many times that amount. And the writer (or team of writers) will earn every penny.

They will spend hours tracking down and interviewing industry experts. They'll have to translate data points and technical jargon into a message that's coherent to a non-technical reader. They'll write multiple drafts that will need to be vetted by various committees.Their facts will be checked and double-checked. And the final paper will have a sophisticated graphic design in keeping with the organization's brand guidelines.

It's a lot of careful work (and expense). But if it results in the kind of document that even a skeptical prospect will think is worth reading, it's all worth it.

Three Reasons To Write Your Own

Lots of white papers are written by people who are not professional writers. They're able to do it because they have a basic grasp of English grammar and they're knowledgeable about their topic. So if you've got those two things going for you, it's not a question of "Can I write my own white paper?" but rather "Why should I write my own white paper?"

Here are a few reasons why.

Budget
You don't have the thousands of dollars it's going to take to hire someone to do it. By writing it yourself, you can save a lot of money.

Authority
Authoring a white paper establishes you as an authority on the subject. Instead of a being known as a guy who sells widgets, you become a resource for information on widgets — someone whose opinions on widgets is worth something.

Knowledge/Experience

Researching and writing a white paper is going to make you better at your job. You're going to have to honestly represent your competition and think like a new client.

Short Time-Frame

You can write one fairly quickly to address issues your prospective customers are facing now. It will take some planning, but you actually can write your own white paper and write it in a single day.

In One Day — Really?

Yes. If you have your sources at hand and use the *White Paper In A Day Template* in this book, you can write a 2,000 word white paper in one day.

However, the "one day" promise works only if you're ready to go.

It's sort of like building a deck in a Saturday. *If* you have your plan, your tools, your lumber, and your hardware all laid out behind your house on Friday night, by the end of the day Saturday you're going to have a deck.

But if on Saturday morning you're heading for the home improvement store, hoping to look at plans and figure out what supplies you'll need, you're probably not going to be BBQing on the new deck by dinner.

To get ready to do your white paper in one day, you'll need to have read this book, figured out your subject, and gotten your authoritative sources in order. You can then plan on a writing your first draft in a single day.

Of course, that's not the version you'll end up sending out. You'll want to send your first draft to your editorial team to get their input. And then you'll need to finalize your formatting and graphics. But the lion's share of the work — getting that first version on paper — will be done.

It's Like Paint By Numbers

The paint-by-numbers craze caught on just after WWII and enjoyed decades of popularity. The promise was this: you could create a nice looking, hand painted work of art for your home with little or no skill. In fact, you could be color blind and still do a nice job on a paint-by-numbers painting.

All you had to do was dab the right color of paint on the right spot.

This is exactly the method you're going to use to write your white paper. I've gone through hundreds of white papers to find dozens of what I believe are the most convincing. By carefully analyzing their argument structure, I have come up with a detailed template, which will guide you paragraph-by-paragraph through writing your own convincing white paper.

I'm giving you a paint-by-numbers canvas. You just need to choose your paint colors and dab them on.

Now the one downside to paint-by-numbers art was if your neighbor got the same kit, you'd end up with identical paintings. That can't happen with this white paper template. At each step you will make content decisions that will differentiate your paper from any others—even if by a 1 in 10,000 chance you pick exactly the same title.

But before we get too far into it, let's make sure we're all talking about the same thing. Here are a few definitions.

What Exactly Is A White Paper Anyway?

A white paper is a document that makes a factual, dispassionate case for a particular action. In business it's used as a marketing tool to persuade decision makers that your kind of company or product makes the most sense. (I say "kind" because you'll see in a minute why a white paper must argue for a *generic* solution.)

The very first white paper is considered to be the 1922 document written by Britain's then Secretary of State Winston Churchill. It outlined a plan for peace in Palestine. Just a few pages long, the paper is well thought out and lays out what seems to be a reasonable solution. Unfortunately, it didn't work.

You will see all kinds of documents claiming to be white papers. But some of them are just articles or opinion pieces formatted to look like white papers. A knowledgeable reader will be able to spot the difference right away. So we want to make sure your paper fits within the generally accepted guidelines.

The Three Major Categories Of White Papers

Most white papers can be labeled as one of the following types.

Backgrounder: Gives the benefits of using a certain product or method, and demonstrates how it fits into and improves the current situation. This kind is often used in conjunction with the launch of a new product.

Numbered List: Presents a set of tips, questions, or points about a certain business issue. It's a great way to grab attention by provocatively introducing a new idea. Example: 7 Things Your Current IT Vendor Doesn't Want You To Know

Problem/Solution: Promises a new solution to a current problem. Like a backgrounder it addresses the current situation. And like the numbered list it sows doubt about competitors (though is much less directly negative). But because it promises to solve a nagging problem, it's more likely to be read by a prospect who doesn't consider himself in the market for the product. This is the kind of white paper you'll be creating.

Today's typical white paper is 6 - 12 pages long (not counting the covers) and can be anywhere from 1,800 words on up. Our *White Paper In A Day Template* will produce a document right around 2,000 words.

A white paper is most effective as a business-to-business communication tool. Or to help consumers make a major financial decision. But people looking for information on toasters or cat food probably won't read one.

The tone of a white paper should be objective not salesy. At the first hint you've dropped your promise to educate the reader, he or she will toss it.

Your white paper should not read like a company web page, blog post, opinion article, brochure, or press release. Unlike the above, it will give a fair and accurate appraisal of methods and products sold by your direct competition—that's why your prospect will want to read it.

But if you structure it properly, your company and product will be an even more convincing choice. You will be the *best* solution, appearing to stand head and shoulders above these other *good* solutions.

Do I Really Need One?

You may be able to write your own white paper, but is that a smart place to be investing your marketing resources? Researching and writing a white paper is a significant investment in time and energy. Maybe that time would be better spent updating your website or setting up a series of email newsletters.

Here are some reasons why a white paper could be worth your effort.

1. You need to reach prospects who wouldn't give your other marketing materials two seconds. Your white paper promises them something they can use even if they never decide to do business with you. Even then, they may only give you three seconds, so make that opening good.

2. Your prospects are holding back for more than relational reasons. They might like you and even trust you personally. But they need something a little more solid to go on. A white paper can give them third party confirmation of the solution you're offering and set you up as a genuine authority in your area of business.

3. Your prospects are constrained by best practices. Your contact likes you and your product, and if it were solely up to them, they'd do business with you. But they need to bring other decision makers onboard. Your white paper can be the evidence they need to gain a consensus decision.

White papers are more widely used in industries that experience rapid change and so decision makers need experts to advise them before they spend millions on something brand new. High tech and software firms have always heavily relied on white papers. But they're appropriate in any industry where change is the norm and you need to establish authority for your new idea.

A white paper will establish authority for your product or service, and for you professionally.

Do I Really Have What It Takes To Write One?

This is a great question to ask yourself before you launch into a major project. You don't want to pour weeks of effort into this only to realize you're not going to end up with a useable document at the end.

You do need basic writing skills but you don't have to be a prolific writer. If you sit down to write a business letter and wonder how you'll ever think of anything important enough to fill up the page, welcome to the club.

To write a white paper you need to be able to compose sentences a little more complex than "See spot run." But not too much. If you think you could write a brief story for the local paper, you'll do fine. In fact, if you're a little critical of your own writing, that's a good sign. The very worst writers are the ones who are blind to their own stylistic flaws. They have no basis for revising their work to make it better.

But you don't have to be able to sit down and dash off 800 words at a sitting. Using our *White Paper In A Day Template* you will never have to compose more than five sentences at a time. So you don't need to be as prolific as Edward Gibbon or Samuel Johnson, or even know who those guys are.

The one thing you will need the whole way through is a strong desire to finish the project. Once you start, there will always be some reason to quit or at least put off the next step and break your project schedule. If you can resist that, you can write your own white paper.

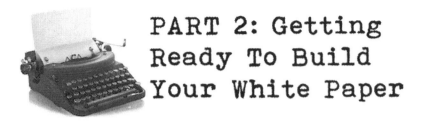

PART 2: Getting Ready To Build Your White Paper

In this section we'll cover the things you'll need to plan for or complete before you sit down to do the actual writing.

Creating A Document To Survive The Snap Judgement

You know how you can size someone up in just a few seconds? We instantly judge people we've just met based on how they dress, how they talk, or how they shake hands. It's usually not fair, but we all do it.

The same thing is going to happen to your white paper, only it'll happen faster. So we want to build it to withstand the initial snap judgement of your readers and pull them in to finish the whole thing.

Using The 3-30-3 Rule

There's a great measure of attention called the 3-30-3 rule. It's a good rule of thumb to keep in mind as you write. A prospect who has enough interest in your white paper to at least look at the cover will first give you **3 seconds**: They will scan the headline to see if it's at all interesting to them.

If it looks compelling, they'll give you about **30 more seconds** as they scan your opening copy. They're most likely not going to read it word-for-word, so you'll want to structure it so they can get your most enticing arguments by skimming.

Then, if your opening succeeds in sucking them in, they'll give you **3 more minutes** of reading. If you can get your prospect to this point, your white paper has found its mark. And she'll want to read it all the way to the end to learn what you recommend.

Basic Structure Of Our White Paper

This book will take you step-by-step through writing a white paper that will conform to the 3-30-3 rule. You'll introduce your argument in such a way that your reader will want to know more. And then you'll lead her along a logical path that ends with your product or service being the best solution.

These are the main sections.

Title
As you can see it's extremely important to have a strong opening, starting with your title. It must strike a nerve with your prospect, talking about a problem that they actually worry about and a plausible solution.

Overview of Your Premise
This will show them in less than 30 seconds that you really understand their problem.

Other Competing Solutions
You'll then describe several solutions that are in direct competition with what you're going to recommend. This will show that you've taken into consideration all viable remedies and aren't just flogging yours.

Your Solution
Next you'll introduce your solution, though you'll need to describe it generically. (I'll explain why when we walk through the actual template.) And you'll detail the major reasons why it's better than the other solutions.

More Problems Solved
You'll present some additional problems solved by your solution, or answers to your reader's most likely objections.

Example
Here you'll give a brief story of a company or person who found success by using your recommended method.

Conclusion
You'll briefly recap how your solution keeps the promise made by your title.

About You
This brief but important section tells who you are, who you work for, and why you're uniquely qualified to author this white paper.

And that's it. Your white paper takes a fairly simple idea, examines it from multiple sides and concludes in favor of your company. At each point you'll quote from published authorities to strengthen your argument.

What's The Proper Writing Style For A White Paper?

As I mentioned earlier, just because a written piece about your company comes out to eight pages that doesn't make it a white paper.

The style or tone of the writing and the citation of outside sources are what will set your white paper apart from other marketing documents.

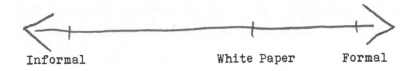

Informal   White Paper   Formal

If we made a scale of writing style where Most Personal/Informal was at the far left and Least Personal/Very Formal was at the far right, a good white paper would be on the right side but not at the very end.

Extremely Formal
This style is reserved for documents with nearly all humanity drained out of them: Contracts, Financial Prospectuses, Quarterly Reports, Instruction Manuals, certain Press Releases, and all kinds of Legal Documents.

Informal
This style is appropriate for documents where you want the personality of the author to come through: Blog Posts, Social Media, Sales Letters, and certain Website Copy.

White Paper Style
Your white paper must engage — so not be completely formal — but it must never directly sell your company. It's like the board game TABOO where certain words (the ones you really want to use) are off limits.

WWTWSJD?

To make sure you maintain the appropriate voice throughout your white paper, you can use this old acting trick. When an actor is playing a character with a completely different accent from his own, it's very easy for that accent to shift during the performance and soon sound nothing like the original character.

So actors use a "touchstone" phrase. It's a line they say to themselves that snaps them back into character and allows them to be consistent from beginning to end.

When writing a white paper, a great touchstone phrase to use is "What would the Wall Street Journal do?"

Imagine the Journal doing a story on your industry. How would they assess the competing methods being put forward by you and your competitors?

They would certainly give every alternative a fair hearing. They would also give the downside to each (including yours). But just imagine that after a fair investigation they found your solution to be the most promising for reasons A, B, and C. That's your white paper right there.

The fact that you're willing to mention the competition and even give them a fair hearing will boost your credibility in your reader's mind. And your use of a serious, journalistic style with third party sources to back up each claim will establish you as an authority.

Opinion pieces, press releases, and letters-from-the-heart can all be effective marketing tools, but don't let their tone slip into your white paper. Leave your personal opinion out and make it unassailably compelling.

Don't Take My Word For It

Journalistic style is heavily dependent on quotations from eyewitnesses and experts. One of the most-used phrases in a news or investigative piece is "according to."

So unlike a brochure, where you can talk at length about your product or business without having to cite other sources, you will need lots of supporting quotes for your white paper. In fact, you really should have a third party source for every assertion you make. Otherwise you're just giving your opinion.

The reason many white papers cost upwards of $4000 is that the writers must track down and interview these expert sources. You won't need to do that if you can find reputable published sources to support your arguments.

If it makes you feel any better, the most challenging part about writing a white paper isn't the writing—it's finding published quotes to back up your arguments.

Three Things To Avoid When You Write

Writing like a professional is so simple. All you have to do is communicate clearly while avoiding obvious errors in style and syntax. That sounds so easy, right?

It's actually not as hard as you think.

When I edit copy for clients, I often come across these three style no-nos. If you can avoid all of them, you'll be well on your way to sounding like a professional writer.

1. Passive Voice
It's when you describe things as just sort of happening instead of saying Who did What to Whom. And it makes it sound like you're trying to cover something up. Corporations and politicians use the passive voice when they're acknowledging some misdeed.

Bad example: We deeply regret that remarks were made that some found offensive.

Should be: Our VP of Marketing referred to some of our maritime customers as "chowderheads." That was wrong. He's been fired.

2. Repeated Wording
In English we don't like to hear the same wording used twice in the same sentence, especially nouns, verbs and their modifiers. If you need to refer to same thing twice, vary your wording the second time.

Example: The city trains run on time, unlike the country trains that don't run on time.

Should be: The city trains run on time, unlike the country trains that don't keep to their schedules.

This also applies to using the same word two sentences in a row. Bad example: Mike tried to go swimming in the lake. But he didn't like how cold it was in the lake. Should be: Mike tried to go swimming in the lake. But he didn't like the cold water.

Only use the exact same wording consecutively if you're purposely going for an effect called parallelism. Sometimes, however, there just isn't another word that's equivalent to you the one you used first. Then it's OK to have two in a row.

3. Clichés, Intellectual Sounding Terms, and Wordiness
These three go together and are often the unfortunate result of "writing like you talk." In conversation we used canned phrases while we're thinking of the next thing to say. But when you're writing and can't think of what comes next, you have the luxury of just putting your pen down until you can figure out the next intelligent thing to say.

To sound like a professional writer, keep these fillers out of your copy.

Clichés are figures of speech that have become worn out with overuse and so now sound insincere.

Example: Let's face it.

Business clichés are just as bad.

Example: It's time to think outside the box.

Another thing to avoid is using recently-coined **industry buzzwords**—especially the kind that are thrown in to try to make the writer sound smart. Consultants might talk like this, but journalists don't write like this (unless they're quoting someone who talks like this).

At best your reader will roll her eyes at your attempt to sound in-the-know. At worst, she won't know what you're talking about and will stop reading.

Finally, avoid **wordiness**. It's good to use all the words you need to describe something. But if there's a shorter way of saying it, that still gets your point across, that's even better. Your editorial team will help you with this.

Gathering Your White Paper Tool Kit

Before you start a big project like sewing a quilt or building a deck, you need to figure out which tools and supplies you need well ahead of time. For the kind of white paper we'll be building, your tool kit will be pretty basic.

Here's the list of what you need.

Your Writing Tools

1. *White Paper In A Day Template*: This is the paragraph-by-paragraph writing guide we'll walk through in this book. It will help you with the the hardest part of your white paper writing — the structure. And it will break your work down into easily doable little parts.

2. *Word Processing Program*: You can use Microsoft Word, Apple Pages, Open Office (a popular free office suite), or even Google Docs (part Google Drive). You just need a good word processing program that can export your document in the PDF format.

3. *Style Guide*: If you have questions about correct English usage, look it up on Google. Don't just rely on what sounds right. Grammar errors in your white paper will seriously hurt your credibility. If you want to be a better writer, before you start, read *The Elements Of Style* by E. B. White (the author of *Charlotte's Web*). It's less than 100 pages and worth more than a whole term of college English.

Your Information Sources

Each time you make an assertion in your white paper you're going to need to back it up with an authoritative source. It's OK to use a single source (i.e., a book or article) more than once. But you're still going to need to find as many as possible that make your exact point. Your sources need to be either published (in a book, magazine, newspaper, or official report) or quoted by a reputable news source.

Or you can go to the trouble of interviewing a respected authority and using his or her quotes. You may also quote this person from his or her official blog. If you do this, it's important that this person not be part of your company. Quoting your own executives will turn your white paper into a press release.

1. *Search Engines*: Just Googling or Binging your subject may turn up a lot of unusable sources like web pages, forum posts, and blog entries by non-experts. So I recommend first using Google News and Bing News searches.

2. *Google Books*: A great way to search the contents of a huge number of books and magazines, and actually get quotes out of them without having to read them all the way through.

3. *Trade Journal Websites*: Identify the leading trade journals for your industry and visit their websites. They will often archive their articles online. Run a few test searches to see if you can find articles to cite.

4. *Some Recommended News Sites*: National Public Radio has a searchable news and article database going back several years at NPR.org. It has a wide array of topics, is authoritative, and free.

5. Both *The Wall Street Journal* and *The New York Times* have exhaustive article databases to search. Many of the articles require a fee to download. But if it's exactly the quote you need, it's more than worth a couple of bucks.

6. *Your Friend The Expert*: If you absolutely cannot find a published source for one or more of your points, it's time to call a friendly expert. This person should be in a related field with some authority to comment on the situation. It's OK to use one of your clients as a source. You just need to quote them talking in general terms, not specifically touting your company.

Your Editorial Team

When you get dressed up for some big, formal event you probably present yourself to a trusted acquaintance and ask, "How do I look?" This person will make sure you don't have food in your teeth, a missed belt loop, or a tag sticking out. You need to do the same with your writing.

We are all blind to our own writing errors. (I'll give you some hints how to minimize this later in the book.) Our brains automatically correct our mistakes in a way that amazes neuroscientists. As a professional writer I'm often tasked with proofing a client's white paper, a brochure that's about to be printed in the thousands, email offers that will be sent out to tens of thousands, and web pages that will be viewed by hundreds of thousands. It's understood that I am not to let the tiniest error slip by — a missing comma, an extra space, a wrong verb tense, a brand name split onto two lines.

By the time I'm done I can guarantee I've caught everything. But I would never dream of sending out my own writing without another editor proofing it. (You'd laugh at my initial mistakes in this book.)

You should have at least two competent people read your white paper after you've gone through and revised it at least once. Ask them to point out any errors in your argument as well as your grammar and spelling. They'll pretend they're doing you a favor. But secretly they'll enjoy finding your errors, since we all love to point out other people's shortcomings.

Your Graphics Resources

You will need a front cover, a back cover, and supporting graphics throughout your white paper. None of these has to be fancy, but they must look professional. Download some white papers to see how different companies handle the layout. For your first effort it's best to keep the design simple and clean. And you can do this basic layout in your word processing program. The body of the paper can just be type with a few images or graphics as illustrations. Hint: Do not use the clip art that comes built-in to your word processing program.

A Graphic Designer: I would strongly recommend hiring a graphic designer to do the graphic layout for your white paper. You can have this done very reasonably and it will boost the credibility of your paper. Even a brilliantly written white paper presented with amateurish, office-party graphics is like sending out an unshaven salesman with a stain on his tie. That's all the prospective customer will see.

Stock Photos & Graphics: You can purchase very professional looking photos, graphics, and illustrations through stock photo sites. Places like iStockPhoto.com and BigStockPhoto.com have tens of thousands of photos and illustrations you can download and use for just a few dollars each. There are many other great stock photo sites as well. Just be careful that the images you purchase are "royalty-free." This means you just pay once. Be sure to read the allowed use agreement before downloading. You're generally free to use the images for any kind of marketing. They just don't want you reselling them.

Do not just grab images off the web without permission. It's unethical and the major photo companies will pursue you with legal action.

You can find free images on the web but they're generally not very good quality and it will take much longer to find something usable. If your time is worth $10 per hour, you're going to come out ahead by going to one of the recommended royalty-free stock photo sites.

Your Calendar

Yes, you need to write some firm dates on your calendar. Set a realistic deadline for your white paper to be ready for distribution. Once you have a date in mind, work backwards to set up a production timeline.

When will you have your Tools together? When is your big writing day? When will you have it to your reviewers? When do you need it back from your graphics people? Projects without dates on the calendar tend to drag on and on.

You need to pick a specific day each stage will be complete, so you can tell if you're behind schedule. This will help you give deadlines to your editorial team and your graphic designer (if you use one). Build in a reasonable amount of time so your finished white paper will have zero mistakes. Once customers have downloaded it, you can't get it back.

With your tools ready to go, it's time to make the first important decision about your white paper. Exactly *who* are you writing this for?

Deciding Who Your Reader Will Be

The more specific the target of your white paper, the more effective it will be. You want the person reading it to be thinking, "Wow, this was written just for me."

To achieve this you need to imagine, as you write it, that it's going to be read by one specific person. It can be a real person or an imaginary one. You just need to have as much detail about them as possible in your mind as you write.

For example: Val is 34 years old. She's owned her own cleaning service for 3 years. Her biggest worry is retaining good employees. She's smart but she doesn't know a lot about X (what you're selling). Etc.

This will help you to decide what to include and what to leave out of your white paper.

You say, "That's fine for Val. But I can't write a separate white paper for each of my prospective customers." You don't have to. The one you write for Val will be appropriate for a lot of your prospects who are small business owners. And once you've written a white paper, it's easy to go through and shift its focus for another kind of prospect.

Tailoring Your White Paper For Various Readers

You won't need to think about this until you've finished your initial white paper. But briefly, it's possible to customize your white paper for a different audience without completely rewriting it.

By changing the title of the paper, the headings, and what's emphasized in the copy you can take one white paper aimed at small business owners and turn it into three more.

For instance, you could tailor it separately for sales, marketing, and operations people. With a new cover for each, because they will each have a new title, they really will be three different papers.

Your only limitation in customizing a single paper into many is making sure they all stay closely related to the same problem/solution. Otherwise, you'll need a whole new argument.

Your Most Important Choice — Your Subject

Your white paper is going to be a well-reasoned argument that leads the reader to conclude that your company is the best solution. But for that to happen you have to start with a subject that's compelling to her.

You can probably list dozens of reasons for clients to go with your product or service. For instance, if they become a customer, you'll regularly take them to lunch. Or their added business will help you pay your son's college tuition. Both are good things, but those aren't your best reasons.

Your white paper must address your clients' highest hopes or greatest fears. You must offer the solution to a problem they really want to solve.

Maybe it's as simple as being well-versed in the marketplace so that when their boss calls on them in a staff meeting, they can give a comprehensive overview and offer the most intelligent solution (hopefully you).

But it must be important enough to them to read about it for 2,000 words.

Ask "The Question"

The topic of your white paper is too important to just make up on your own. If this part isn't right, all your efforts afterwards will be a waste.

The question you want to ask is, "Why do our clients choose us?"

You might already have a good sense of what this is. Great. But you need second, third, and fourth opinions just to make sure.

Here are some people to ask:
- Your sales staff
- Your newest clients
- Your loyal clients
- Your support staff
- Someone who refers customers to you

And then *do* ask yourself. Take the time to think about and write down why clients choose you.

After taking all of the above into consideration, choose the strongest reason from your clients' perspective as the subject for your white paper.

What If I End Up With 3 Great Reasons?

You still have to pick just one. But now you have the subjects for your next two white papers.

PART 3:
Building Your
White Paper

We will now go step-by-step through building your white paper.

Please read this all the way through before starting. Yes, we all love trying to put bikes, BBQs, and IKEA shelves together without reading the directions first. But trust me, doing this will save you extra work later.

The white paper you're going to build has 14 major parts. Each of those has a few sub parts. It's been broken down so that at each step in the building process you only have to come up with one citation and one or two paragraphs of copy. (If you didn't know, "copy" is what advertising and journalism people call the text. Back in the old days it indicated that the writing was to be printed or copied.)

What Do You Mean By "Length"?
Under each little section I'll give you a suggested length in number of words for each block of copy. For instance, your description of the current situation should be about 60 words. Think of it as a minimum to get you to your 2000 word total. If you need to make that part longer or a little shorter, feel free to do so. The goal is to make your argument flow smoothly.

Creating Your Shopping List
You're going to need at least 9 citations to build your white
paper. Once you know what your topic and argument will be,
read through the following outline and make a "shopping list"
of the kinds of published quotes you'll need. Then you'll fill
that list when you visit your online news, trade journal, and
official report websites. As you go through the outline, you'll
see what I mean.

Before you do any writing, you need to hunt down these
citations and have them printed out or kept in a plain text file
for easy copy/paste when you're composing.

My promise of a white paper in a day only works if you have
your authoritative quotations ready to go.

To Footnote Or Not To Footnote

Some white paper authors footnote all of their sources. They
have a little superscript number like this[1]. And then at the
bottom of the page or at the end of the paper in teeny tiny
print they have the same number with the citation's source
listed according to rules of research papers.

It's not necessary for you to do this. In fact, footnotes at the
bottom of the page interrupt the flow of the reading. So if you
have to use them, they should go at the very end of the paper.

Otherwise, you can avoid having to use them by simply
identifying the source for your quotes in the body of the copy
and then keeping the full listing on file in case somebody
wants to look them up.

Now you're ready to walk through the plan for your white
paper.

Going Through The *White Paper In A Day Template*

The following is like the recipe for writing your own white paper. At each point I'll give you some notes and an example.

The plain *White Paper In A Day Template*, without the editorial comments, is included at the end of this book. (See the final **Note To The Reader** section to get additional versions of the template.)

Step 1. Create Your Title

This is *the* most important part of your white paper. You've got 3 seconds to hook your reader. Your title must grab your prospect by the lapels and say, "I know what your biggest problem is and I have your solution."

Take your subject and write it in the form of a Problem/Solution statement.

Here are some examples. (Note: I'm putting the example copy in italics. You, of course, won't do your whole white paper in italics.)

Ant Infestations In Food Preparation Areas: The Non-Toxic Way To Get Rid Of Them

Low Price Online Retailers: How To Beat Them With Your Bricks-And-Mortar Store

Employee Turnover: Compete To Keep Your Best Workers Without Increasing Payroll Costs

Untested Managers: Get Them Up And Running With Real World Experience In One Day

The format here is Bad News/Good News. If you like crime dramas you can think of it as Bad Cop/Good Cop. Just be sure you can deliver on the Good News part of your title.

How long should your white paper title be? The shorter and punchier the better. It has to make sense in a single glance. More words here will not give you more attention. Do *not* write something like this:

Your Competitors Have More Salespeople Than You With Bigger Expense Accounts And Advertising Budgets: But Here's A Pretty Good Way To Outsell Them And Get A Better Quality Customer Without Spending The Kind Of Money They're Spending On An Annual Basis

You get the idea.

Step 2. Write A Two Sentence Summary Of The Problem/Solution

Length: 30 words

Your prospect gave you 3 seconds and read your headline. And, congratulations, she wants to know more. Now you've got about 30 seconds to set the hook. You'll do this with a two sentence summary of your target's problem and your promised solution.

Here are three examples.

When the health inspector finds ants in a commercial kitchen, the owner can face fines or even closure. But the latest advances in pest control can eliminate the infestations without the use of toxins.

Losing key employees can seriously affect a business's customer service. But money alone won't keep the best team members from moving on to greener pastures.

Employers who provide a 401(k) plan for their employees can be personally liable for excess fees as well as the plan's performance. Fortunately, the Department of Labor has several ways to significantly reduce this risk.

Step 3. (A B C) Write A Brief Summary Of Your White Paper's Premise

Here's where you fully lay out the problem. Hopefully, your reader will see that you know what you're talking about and want to read the rest of the paper to see how you solve it.

3 A) Write two sentences that describe the current situation.

Length: 40 words

Example:
For many generations the local hardware store has enjoyed an all-but-guaranteed stream of business in small communities. Patrons have been willing to pay higher prices for personalized service and to save the time and expense of driving to an urban chain store.

3 B) Write two or three sentences on recent factors that are affecting the current situation.

Length: 60 words

Example:

The rise of the internet and the expansion of big box home improvement stores to the fringes of suburban areas has changed that. Now customers can order directly from home or if they need an item immediately (in the case of a plumbing repair), they can drive a short distance and get a much better selection and lower prices than their local hardware store.

3 C) Write three sentences on how this has become a major problem for the reader.

Length: 80 words

Example:
As a result, local hardware retailers are facing significant competition where it didn't exist before. A 3,000 square foot store can't stock the hundreds of thousands of items available online. And on the weekends, when they get their most traffic, they can't match the prices of the big box retailers just a short drive away. If a local hardware store owner in this situation continues business-as-usual, he will soon be out of business.

Notice that we didn't use any external citations in this overview. We just laid out the situation. In the next sections, as we demonstrate why our premise is true, we'll back up our assertions with authoritative sources.

4. (A B C) Give The Evidence For The Problem

You will now begin using your authoritative quotes to lay out the problem in detail.

4 A) Write a six sentence paragraph where you describe an example of the problem and give a citation.

Length: 140 words

I won't give you a full example here because you're starting to get the idea. You need to find a published source (or a person you know who's an independent authority) that talks directly about one aspect of the problem. It will sound better if you set up the quote with a sentence describing the problem.

Then introduce the quote with something like: *According to Hardware Age Magazine, independent retailers are seeing a decline in in-store sales.*

Quote several lines of your source using quotation marks: *"Independent hardware stores have seen a decline in same store sales for the third straight year . . . etc."*

Then add a summary of additional information from the source: *The article also states that rural retailers are being hit harder than suburban stores, many of which are seeing growth.*

Remember that publication titles like *The Wall Street Journal* should be in italics. Same for books. Be sure to give your source full credit for the quote. List the month and year for a newspaper or magazine. Give the title and author of a book. Give the full title for a web-only article. The idea is that your reader should be able to look up any of your sources if she wants to.

Finally, conclude with a sentence of your own, summing up the assertion: *The picture looks bleak for stores hoping to do business the traditional way.*

4 B) Write a six sentence paragraph where you describe another aspect of the problem.

Length: 140 words

Find a source that addresses a second part of the problem.

You'll need a transition sentence to set up this additional aspect.

Example:
But local retailers are also facing a significant challenge on a second front — online sales.

Then set up, cite, and summarize your quote the same way you did for 4A.

5. (A, B) Straw Solution 1

Here is where you will give alternatives to your solution a fair hearing. Well, sort of fair. You ultimately want your idea to win out.

I call this a "Straw Solution" after the straw man logical fallacy. That's where you don't acknowledge the strongest version of your opponent's argument, but you present a weaker version that's easier to knock down.

In our hardware store example, one of your straw solutions to losing business to online retailers might be to enact a local internet sales tax. It's probably not going to solve the problem but localities have tried this and you can cite it as an example.

5 A) Write two or three sentences describing your straw solution.

Length: 60 words

Your description should give this idea a serious treatment. It will make your argument more convincing when one of your experts knocks this straw solution down.

5 B) Quote an expert on why this solution isn't practical.

Length: 70 words

Broadcast news uses this style of argument all the time. They give what sounds like a fair airing of an idea, but then they give the last word to an expert who disagrees and pokes major holes in it. On any topic you can always find an expert who disagrees.

6. (A, B) Straw Solution 2

You're now going to bring up another solution, that's not yours, that on the surface sounds really good. In fact, it should sound better than Straw Solution 1.

6 A) Write two or three sentences describing Straw Solution 2.

Length: 60 words

6 B) Quote an expert on why this solution isn't practical.

Length: 70 words

7. (A, B, C) Introduce The Real Solution

Now you get to talk about *your* solution to the problem, the one you're hoping to convince the reader is the real one. It's near and dear to your heart, but just like with your straw solutions, let your experts make your case. You're reporting "just the facts, ma'am."

7 A) Write three sentences explaining what the real solution is.

Length: 70 words

7 B) Write four sentences explaining why the real solution is better than Straw Solution 1 and Straw Solution 2.

Length: 90 words

7 C) Quote an expert on why it's better than the Straw Solutions.

Length: 30 words

8. (A, B, C) Explain How The Real Solution Addresses Major Concern 1

You are now going to go beyond the introduction and explanation of your better solution. You are going to explain how it addresses other major problems.

You can probably think of 10 reasons why your method is better than the competition. You need to pick the top 3 and then find expert quotes to back them up.

8 A) Write one sentence introducing Major Concern 1.

Length: 30 words

8 B) Write four sentences explaining how the real solution addresses this concern.

Length: 90 words

8 C) Give an expert citation to support this argument.

Length: 30 words

9 (A, B, C) Explain How The Real Solution Addresses Major Concern 2

9 A) Write one sentence introducing Major Concern 2.

Length: 30 words

9 B) Write four sentences explaining how the Real Solution addresses this concern.

Length: 90 words

9 C) Give an expert citation to support this argument.

Length: 30 words

10 (A, B, C) Explain How The Real Solution Addresses Major Concern 3

10 A) Write two sentences introducing Major Concern 3.

Length: 30 words

10 B) Write four sentences explaining how the Real Solution addresses this concern.

Length: 90 words

10 C) Give an expert citation to support this argument.

Length: 30 words

11. An Example Of A Company Or Client Succeeding With The Real Solution

Write five sentences, telling the story of someone who used your solution to solve the major problem in your title.

Length: 125 words

It would be best if you can find an example of this in a published source. If you can't, you can use one of your clients. But you should avoid mentioning your company. The danger here is that you will drop out of your white paper voice into your sales voice.

So if you use one of your own clients as an example, leave yourself out of it and don't use "we."

12. (A, B, C) Give Three More Advantages Of The Real Solution

Your solution is so good, it has lots of advantages. Here are three more. These can be more solutions to problems or just positive results from using your method. You only need a citation for the last one.

12 A) Write five sentences describing Advantage 1.

Length: 125 words

12 B) Write five sentences describing Advantage 2.

Length: 125 words

12 C) Write six sentences describing Advantage 3.

Length: 175 words

Make this the best of the three Advantages. And then add a citation to bolster this point (adding another 25 words).

13. Recap The Problem/Real Solution Argument

Length: 50 words

End the white paper with a recap of the problem and how we've just seen it can be best solved. Make your last sentence a strong suggestion about what the prospect should do.

14. (A, B, C, D) Information About The Author

Length: 70 words

These four sentences will establish your expertise.

A. Bob Smith is _____ (current title) at _____ (name of company) where he _____ (does something).

B. Prior to that he _____ (did something).

C. Bob is also _____ (another current thing you're doing).

D. (Name of Company) provides _____ (whatever your company does)

D. Phone and email contact.

And that's it for the writing part. When you look at it in little pieces, it doesn't seem like such an overwhelming task.

Now you're ready to start the actual work.

PART 4: Doing The Writing

You're now ready to begin your work.

Plan Your Timeline

Before you do anything else you need to get out your calendar and **plan the schedule** for building your white paper.

Decide What Your Paper Is Going To Be about

Next, you need to **choose your subject**, following the method in *Part 2: Getting Ready To Build Your White Paper*.

Once you have that, go back through the Template and **decide on your main points**. You don't have to have any wording. Just know what you will be arguing at each point, e.g., 3 A), 3 B), 3C), etc.

Finally, go to your information resources and **fill your shopping list** with the authoritative quotes you'll need to bolster your argument.

These three may take a little time. But that's fine. You want to make sure that when you start writing, you're going in the right direction.

Your Writing Day

When you have your subject, your supporting citations, and a basic idea of what your argument will be, you're ready to write your white paper in one day.

In your writing schedule set aside an actual day (or two half days) to do this. You're going to need uninterrupted time to get your brain into writing mode, find your white paper voice, and get your ideas flowing.

In other words, every time you sit down to write, it's going to take time to find your focus.

That's why, in my experience, I can get more writing done in a single five-hour chunk of time than in five one-hour sessions.

Plan To Deal With Distractions

If there's a Murphy's Law for writing, it would be: The minute you sit down to write, distractions will swarm from the woodwork.

The room will be too hot. It'll be too cold. It'll be too noisy. It'll be too quiet. You'll suddenly get the strong impression that someone is urgently trying to get ahold of you on Facebook chat.

You may need to sequester yourself somewhere where there are fewer interruptions. You need to mute your phone, shut off all social media, and not give in to the temptation to check your email every 15 minutes.

Some people (like me) are more easily distracted than others. I will often go somewhere with just a pen and a spiral notebook to get my first draft down on paper. I find that I can think faster than I can write and that keeps the pump primed. After that, typing it into a computer and revising it are easy.

But if you're comfortable composing straight into your computer, do that.

Take Little Bites

When faced with a blank piece of paper or a blank computer screen, it's tempting to do something else — anything else than write. We think how hard it's going to be to compose all those pages and pages of copy.

That's why the *White Paper In A Day Template* we're following breaks the writing down into easily doable little pieces. You don't have to think about writing 2,000 words. You just think about your next three sentences.

Don't Edit, Write

On your first draft, you should just let the words flow out. Don't stop to rewrite. Of course you should cross out or delete any mistakes, but concentrating on getting the basic wording out.

If you try to perfect each sentence after you write it, you'll lose your momentum. And writer's block is when you freeze up because you can't think of anything good enough to put on paper. Just try to get it all down according to the template.

You can fix it later.

Go For It

Write the complete first draft of your white paper. Make sure you've done each step in the template and it's completely typed into your computer.

Now you're ready to give to give it a professional polish.

The One Thing Nobody Wants To Do

The secret to good writing, that nobody likes to do, is REVISE. It can be discouraging to think that after all that work have to do some of it over again.

We prefer to think that our writing is like the Greek goddess Athena, who sprang fully mature from Zeus's head. It's not. The very best writing that flows effortlessly has been revised numerous times.

Because you have organized your writing according to a proven structure, chances are you'll have big sections of your paper that only need minor editing. But to make it its best, you need to carefully go through it several times.

However, if you plan your revisions as part of the process, it's not so bad.

Polishing Your First Draft

Once you have your first complete draft written, read it all the way through, making sure you're not missing any words and the transitions between your major points make them flow together into one cohesive argument.

Next, read it aloud. This will allow you to see errors that don't stand out when you read it silently. Print out your white paper, grab a pencil, and go somewhere where you can read it aloud without being overheard. Pretend you're presenting it like a speech to a group.

Or, actually record yourself like you're reading a book on tape. You can use the voice recorder on your smartphone. Then listen to yourself on your way home from work.

In both cases, if you read your first draft with feeling, you're going to hear where it needs revisions. And that's why you need a paper copy with you, so you can pause and quickly note the parts that need help.

Again, because the Template has given you a good structure to follow, you probably won't need to make the major changes that can be so discouraging.

Get Ready To Make Headlines

Now that you've revised your first draft, it's time to add headlines to your copy. These will help introduce each new section and guide the reader if he or she is just skimming.

Make these headlines short and to the point. They should pique your prospect's interest, making her curious to read more.

Examples:

The Growing Problem

Demographic Challenges

A New Solution

Where To Put Your Headlines

You can insert a headline anywhere you think it's appropriate. They have two jobs. One is to break up your copy so it looks easier to read. (If it looks like too much work, people won't read it.) The other is to set up the next section of your white paper.

I suggest using them to introduce the following six sections.

4. Evidence Of The Problem

5. Straw Solutions

7. The Real Solution

8. Real Solution Addresses Major Concerns

11. Example Company Succeeding

12. Final 3 Advantages

With your headlines in place, it's reading like a real white paper. Now it's time to pass it along to your Editorial Team.

PART 5: Getting Your White Paper Ready To Go

You'll now begin the process of first polishing the copy and after that's done, doing your layout and graphics.

Submit It To Your Editorial Team — With Instructions

As you recall, your Editorial Team is a group of people whose opinion you trust. They should be from within your organization or a trusted partner or vendor. You should also get their permission ahead of time to use them as a resource for this. Because you want them to take the time to carefully read your white paper. Not just skim it.

Give your team a specific deadline to get your white paper back in a timely manner.

When you send them your first draft, give specific directions on the kind of critique you're looking for.

Tell them the specific goals for your paper:
1. It's a white paper, so it should have an impartial journalistic tone.
2. It's supposed to convey the best argument for your company or product without falling into sales language.
3. It should hook the reader at the beginning and lead them all the way through to the end.

Then ask them to please let you know where, in their opinion, it's not doing these things.

I've found that if you just ask people what they think about a piece of writing, they will simply tell you all the things they don't like about it — even if there isn't really anything wrong with it. If you don't give them specific things to look for (your goals for the piece), they're tempted to just validate themselves as a critic.

Make Your Final Revisions To The Copy

Be sure to collect all the input from your editorial team. Then look carefully at what they've noted. If two or more of them point out the same thing, you might strongly consider making that change. But you don't have to follow everyone's advice on the edits. You're the author. Make the revisions you think are valid then read your white paper aloud again.

When the copy is ready to go, you can add the graphics.

Branding Your White Paper And Inserting Graphics

The term "branding" used to mean putting your mark on your cow. Since then it's come to mean the whole arsenal of strategies for defining and telling your company's story through words and graphics. In fact, the term has become so broad, it can mean just sticking your logo on something.

We're back to the cow.

So when I say "branding your white paper," I don't mean poking it with a hot iron. I mean "just make it look like it came from your company." This is especially important on the front and back covers, and to a lesser extent inside.

Some companies like to have their logo on every page of their white papers. I don't think it's necessary for you to do that on this first one, since your information is all over the covers and in the About The Author section.

If you haven't already, download some white papers to see what kind of design you like. I suggest clean and simple for your first time out. Keep the "white" in white paper.

Earlier we talked about getting graphic elements like stock photos to illustrate and break up the text. Of course, you want to find images that look like they have something to do with your topic.

If your white paper is about improving warehouse safety, find shots of guys on forklifts and shots of people who look like managers consulting their clipboards. If your first search on the big stock photo sites doesn't get you what you need, keep searching with alternate wording. They have a photo of just about anything you can think of.

Once you have the images you want, get them ready for insertion in your white paper.

In your word processing program insert appropriate images at three or four major points in your document. Place them right below your headlines. Size the images so they're not too large. They shouldn't dominate the pages.

Get Help From A Graphic Designer

If you're on a tight budget or are knowledgeable about graphic design, you can create your covers and do the layout of your white paper yourself. Otherwise, I would strongly suggest farming out this part to a graphic designer.

He or she can help you choose the best typefaces, font sizes, positions for your photos, as well as output your white paper in your preferred format. For instance, it's ideal if you can get it as a Word document with the graphics embedded so you can still make small revisions to the copy on your own.

Then you can easily export if for distribution as a PDF file.

PART 6:
Distributing
Your White Paper

With your white paper written, revised, and laid out with graphics, it's time to get it in front of as many prospects as possible.

It's Ready To Go — Almost

I know I said you'd be done by now. But in my experience, it's common for a client to spot an error at this stage that somehow got by everybody else.

After your layout and graphics are done, give your paper one more careful read-through. Seeing it in its final form will reveal any places in the copy that need a little tweaking. It should look like a unified whole with headlines, images, and copy all flowing in the same direction.

It's a great feeling to see your white paper at this stage. Now you get to share it with others.

But not the whole world quite yet.

You only have one chance to make a first impression. So even though *you're* happy with your white paper, don't immediately post it to your website.

Send it back to your editorial team so they can see the fruits of their labor, and then send it to a few trusted colleagues who have not seen it at all before. Ask them for their impressions and to let you know if they spot any errors.

Again, you may not want to follow any of their suggestions, but you'll at least have some feedback from a test audience.

OK, you're finally ready to send it out as a PDF. Here are some ideas for doing that.

Ideas For Distribution

These are some of the most common ways companies distribute their white papers. As you get into this process you're going to think of more on your own.

Your Website
Create a page devoted entirely to this white paper. List the main benefits of reading it. Make it easy to download. Promote this page on your homepage and any other page that gets a lot of traffic.

Sales Staff
They should be sending it to their current prospects, either emailing the link to your white paper web page or mailing out a color printed copy. Your salespeople should also take printed copies to leave with prospects after face-to-face meetings.

Social Media
Post about your new white paper on Facebook, Twitter, Google+, Pinterest, your blog, and any forums you're a member of. Then mention it again as you get good reactions, noting the positive responses..

You don't want to browbeat your followers, so come up with creative ways to work in ongoing mentions. For instance, link to an article that talks about a point you make in the white paper and mention this.

Your Email List

Send a special message announcing your new white paper. Have it link to your white paper download page. (Don't ever email the PDF as an attachment to your whole list. This will trip all kinds of virus warnings.) After your initial announcement, continue to mention the white paper in your regular email newsletters.

Marketing Partners

If you team up with other firms for marketing, ask them to distribute your white paper.

Related Email Lists

Ask friends with related businesses to offer your white paper as a resource in their email newsletter. They can mention it and then have a link to your landing page for easy downloading.

Trade Shows And Conferences

If you go to trade shows or conferences, bring printed copies to hand out.

Public Speaking And Webinars

Your white paper can be the basis for speaking engagements. Apply to be a presenter at a trade show, conference, or online webinar. Then get permission to distribute it to your attendees.

Employee Education

Your white paper can be a great tool for educating your own employees. And once they know about it, they will think of other people who should see it.

It Gets Easier Each Time

Once you've written and distributed your first white paper, you're going to realize "that wasn't so hard." And hopefully, experiencing the benefits of this powerful marketing tool will encourage you to write more.

When you've authored just one white paper, you've established yourself as an authority on that subject. Even if nobody ever reads it (highly unlikely) but just skims through to see that you're the author, you are likely to be contacted as a trusted resource.

And isn't that the whole point of writing a white paper, anyway?

Get Started Today

If you've just read this through for the first time, you're ready to go. Now you can go back and start planning your subject, the kinds of arguments you want to make, and your production calendar.

You *can* write your white paper in one day. And soon you'll be enjoying the benefits of this powerful marketing tool, and your new authority as an author.

So get started on your planning today.

Special Note To The Reader Who Gets This Far

The fact that you're reading this note at the end impresses me for one of two reasons:
A) You read the book all the way through.
B) You skipped to the end just to see what this note says.

Either way, you showed initiative. And that's the quality that's most important for writing your first white paper. You've never done it before. It seems a little intimidating. But having initiative means you jump right in anyway.

As your reward for making it back here, I want to offer you further white paper writing resources.

- A white paper I wrote using this book.

- The *White Paper In A Day Template* as a PDF file.

- Information on my *How To Write A White Paper In One Day* video course that expands on what's here in the book.

Just email me at brian@brianboys.com and put "Note To The Reader" in the subject line. I'll send you links to all of the above.

Again, thanks for reading this book. I hope you found it useful.

~Brian

White Paper In A Day Template
Create A 2000 Word Problem/Solution White Paper

1. Your title in the form of a reader's problem/reader's solution premise

2. One sentence summary of problem/solution (30 words)

3. Overview of white paper's premise
A. The current situation (40 words)

B. Has led through these steps (60 words)

C. To this major problem for the reader (80 words)

(Insert headline here)

4. Evidence of the problem
A. Example 1 with citation (140 words)

B. Example 2 with citation (140 words)

(Insert headline here)

5. Straw Solution 1
A. Describe solution briefly (60 words)

B. Expert quote on why it doesn't work (70 words)

6. Straw Solution 2
A. Describe solution briefly (60 words)

B. Expert quote on why it doesn't work (70 words)

(Insert headline here)

7. Introduce Real Solution
A. Explain what it is (70 words)

B. Explain why it's better than Straw Solution 1 and Straw Solution 2 (90 words)

C. Expert quote on why it's better (30 words)

(Insert headline here)

8. Real Solution Addresses 1st Major Concern
A. Introduce Concern 1 (30 words)

B. How the Real Solution addresses it (90 words)

C. Citation to support this (30 words)

9. Real Solution Addresses 2nd Major Concern
A. Introduce Concern 2 (30 words)

B. How the Real Solution addresses it (90 words)

C. Citation to support this (30 words)

10. Real Solution Addresses 3rd Major Concern
A. Introduce Concern 3 (30 words)

B. How the Real Solution addresses it (90 words)

C. Citation to support this (30 words)

(Insert headline here)

11. One example of a company or individual succeeding with the Real Solution (125 words)

(Insert headline here)

12. 3 more advantages of the Real Solution
A. Advantage 1 (125 words)

B. Advantage 2 (125 words)

C. Advantage 3. Make this the best of the three (175 words)

And include a citation for this final one (25 words)

13. Recap the Problem/Real Solution argument (50 words)

14. About the Author section (70 words)

A. Bob Smith is _____ (current title) at _____ (name of company) where he _____ (does something).

B. Prior to that he _____ (did something).

C. Bob is also _____ (another current thing you're doing).

D. (Name of Company) provides _____ (whatever your company does)

D. Phone and email contact.

About The Author

Brian Boys is a freelance writer with more than 25 years of experience in marketing for companies of all sizes. He began his career as an advertising agency copywriter, winning awards for print, radio, and TV. He has worked on every conceivable writing project from product naming to book manuscripts, and now primarily writes long-form content for clients in a variety of industries. Find out more at BrianBoys.com/about

You can contact him at brian@brianboys.com

Made in the USA
Middletown, DE
06 November 2019